MORE Bright and Shiny THINGS

a book of poetry by
AmyLee

Also by AmyLee

Bird with a Bright Object

Copyright © 2024 by AmyLee

All rights reserved.
No portion of this book may be reproduced in any form without written permission from the publisher or author, except as permitted by U.S. copyright law.

Cover Artwork and Design by Katherine Magpie Design

Interior Design by Jourdan Dunn

Table of Contents

Dedication
Foreword

How I Poem

My Body of Work	1
The Delicious Burden of Research	3
Spinning Straw into Poems	4
It's Not Just the Words	5
Restoration	6
Tease	8
The Perpetual Idea Machine	9
Turmoil	10
Writer's Wraith	11

I Crossed the Pond

I Spoke with Strangers	15
The Chimneys of Great Britain	16
The Great Unknown	17
Forgiveness, River	18
If You Love Me	19
Old Souls	20
Squirrel King	21
Signposts	22
Words In Mouth	24
I Am Stardust	26
The Wild Thing	27
Shakespeare's Garden	28

Flights of Fancy

Concerning Pixies	33
Chalice and Knightly Code	35
Emblazoned Favors	37
The Cussing Monk	39
Desolate Wilderness of the Mind	40
Nightmare Carousel	41
Submitted for Your Inspection	42
Left to Ashes	44
Sat on the Curb	45
Transient Dreams	47

Memento Mori

Puccini's Tables	51
Deluxe Between the Lines	53
Old Woman	54
Winding Time	56
Lost Days and Found	58
Soliloquy for the Dead	60
Her Soul's Journey	62
Paper Cranes	64
On the Precipice	66

Spells, Dreams, Incantations

I've Drawn Down the Moon	69
Moving Pencils	70
My Divination	72
Clairvoyant's Bend	74
Grind	75
I don't Shy Away	76
Making Memory Work	77
Light Worker Ways	79
Seanchaí to the Spirits	81

Music Memory

David Bowie	85
Transistor Sister Radio	87
Bad Brains	88
1970s Speakers	90
Patti Smith's Words	92
Stella by Starlight	94
Necessity: Come Worship at the Altar of the Eccentric	95

True Love's Kiss

Are You There	99
He Manifests	101
A Dream for the Young and Inclined	103
Spaces Between Us	105
The Pleasure of Your Company	106
Come Down to the River	107

Heart, Soul, and Mind

Eager Mornings	111
Aging	113
Defiance	114
Rebellious Heart	115
Skitter	116
Whim	117
Wine Glass	118
Golden Opportunities	119
Infatuated Girl	121
The Knell of Electric Death	122
Finding Balance	124
Out of Dog Food	125
Wolf Thanksgiving	128
The Sorry State of Utility	130
Highways of Kindness	131
Every Sort of Midnight	132

Inventory of a Human Being   134

Childhood's Reflection

How Long, Not Long   139
Loneliness and Imagination   141
Birds and Bees   142
Fourth of July   144
Summer Evenings   146
Expecting Company   148
Breathe In   150

Mother Earth

Soon Transformed   155
Blackbirds   156
How a Fish Sees   157
Sweeping the Clouds   159
Brooding Balance   161
Ashes Scattered   162
Season's Cycle   163
Dandelion   165
Rainbow Elegance   166
Songs of the Birds   168
Graceless   169
Red Tailed Hawks   171
Sensible Flowers   173
Sweet Refreshment   174
Rock in the Riverbed   175
Underwater Shimmer   176
Offerings   178

Author's Note
Acknowledgements
About the Author

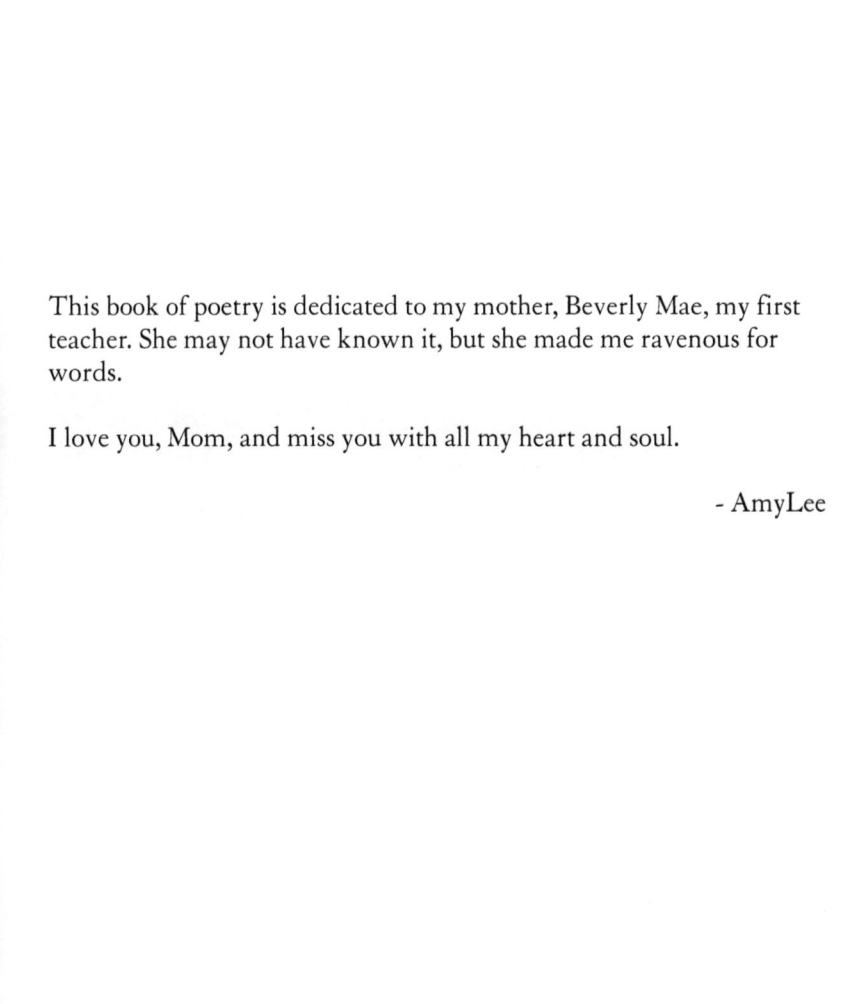

This book of poetry is dedicated to my mother, Beverly Mae, my first teacher. She may not have known it, but she made me ravenous for words.

I love you, Mom, and miss you with all my heart and soul.

- AmyLee

As a touring musician and published author, I've worked with some of New Zealand's best and most well-known poets, hearing them night after night, reciting their work with amazing passion, emotion, and power. And what is a song anyway, but a poem set to music?

I first found AmyLee's poem posted on Twitter/X for the world to enjoy. Her words immediately resonated and I have since read nearly everything of hers I could find. The poetry recognized something within me.

AmyLee's poems are personal, raw, real, and brave. They touch me deeply and I think they will reach you, too. I agreed to write this foreword and it is a formidable task to pen something that must match the skill and emotion within these following pages.

I hope you love these beautiful poems as much as this old rocker does.

- David Owen Thompson

How I Poem

My Body of Work

I have prayed
for my voice to be heard
throat chakra wide open
vocal cords vibrating
LAY
IT
BARE
this splendid repast on life's table
with carving knives and bloody entrails
not the body of Christ
my body of work
and I beseech you
I want to scream my lungs out
open my mouth
let sound fly where it will
hear my plea, angels of the universe
for safety and comeuppance
reassurance validate me
and let me validate myself
feedback, an endless loop
I
AM
BEGGING
but
I. REFUSE. TO. BEG.
even when fear of reprisal
may crush me
I
WILLINGLY
PAY
because freedom is terrifying
and sublime.
I am not the awfulness of my repression

the journey
and blessings
begin where I stand
with back straight and resolve solid
I have bled for this.

The Delicious Burden of Research

Research is a quest
the painstaking effort
I'm willing to put forth
turn me on
an unadulterated thrill
treasure maps
arduous treks
unending tasks
make me hot and bothered
the sort
when I begin to feel lost
and I'm just about
to rip out my hair
scream and vent
only then does it become
crystal clear
I'm approaching nirvana
my Shangri-La
the feeling I get when I break down
castle doors
notebooks and pens
serve as my weapons
then climax is close
and neurosis at its finest
laborious intent
an orgasm of information
sometimes makes me wish
I still smoked.

Spin Straw into Poems

Pray.
My life
depends upon it.
Spin.
Straw into gold
and grant me
all of you old gods
just one more day
to make my mark.
I promise, I promise
to do what I can
with the mess of my brain
and my contrary notions
find that hidden closet
at the back of the house
where the coins are stacked
and none too neat.
I'll mine those words
as they lay quiet in piles
and draft
pretty phrases
illuminating my soul
in a different light
than what I feel today
and may those words take wing
into something poetic
and rival the beauty
I do not possess
and rally the strength
I wish that I had.

It's Not Just the Words

It's not just the words
but the placement, the order
not just the lines
but the length, the look, the feel on the page
then there are the dashes, the commas, etc.
all caps or none whatsoever
the choice is yours -
you stand on the edge of a razor
it all depends
on the choices you've made.

It's not just the syllables
but how they flow together
here are a few - have a listen if you please
noisy or whispered
it's how they're presented
dandelion fluff
echoey brick wall
or metallic clang
choose and choose wisely.

It's not just the touches, tastes, or smells
those are the things you know so well
the rhymes and rhythms
are of great import
but not as keen as the overall thing
and how you felt when you sat down
the day you found the words and wrote them free
and rolled them on your tongue
between your fingers
birthed from your mind
those are the days - sublime, divine.

Restoration

The breath of poetry—
kindling waiting for a match
life's pulsation
lush and bountiful
deep, cleansing
inhale and exhale
awaiting next thoughts
and then the next—

Stored up tears, unaware
and the righteous anger
the velocity of which terrifies.

Examine a thousand
lives that never were
or should have been
or are right now
or used to be.

The lens of an insightful
microscope more powerful
than I could fathom—
pictures at an exhibition
all on display
for the wary and the weary
for the joyful and the innocent
raw life jumps
from paper
trapped impatiently behind glass
that begs breaking.

Poetry paints me with colors and textures
I hid from, like clothing I wished for—

worried how I would look when I wore it
out to dinner with the family.

—Restoration takes
courage and pain and vision.

I aim to take
broadest brushstrokes and render finest detail
and recreate—me.

Tease

Tease me -
as I turn the pages
begin the adventure
the mystery, the tale
the idea of
what might come to be
gives me a thrill
a new story
an idea
a clue -
your dreams
and how you view the world
I want to know everything about you
because I find human beings
to be fascinating
singular yet similar
in our wants and needs
you need not tell me all of it now
I will wait with unmitigated patience
draw it out
make the story longer
that's fine with me
I love to look forward
to your words and voice and feelings.

I open the book -
Will you tease me?

The Perpetual Idea Machine

The brain
a perpetual
idea machine
a nervous meandering
churning,
seething,
and roiling
with thoughts
so easily distracted
by birds and squirrels
then focus, focus
get back to the draft
or the bills
or the thought
what was the thought
where are my keys
when did I eat last
and was it delicious
did I buy laundry soap
why does my head ache
oh! birds!

The brain, a perpetual idea machine.

Turmoil

When my thoughts dance
a wild and fiendish gyre
they whirl unsettled
and the disquietude
can be endured
not a moment more.

What shall I do to salve
this terrible inner turmoil?
How shall I calm
the darkness of my savage creature?

Deliverance, it is hoped, may be
within the words - within the lines.

Writer's Wraith

Ink stains fingers
nail-beds aching and ragged
bleed out of my soul
day in, day out
to the ends of comprehension

A craving -
for light and tallow and bulbs
flickering stench and incandescent
feathers and quills
fountain pens
pencils sharpened with rusty knives
lamb skin, vellum, parchment, rag laid, wood pulp
- never quenched

Devils beseech
typewriter, desktop, laptop, tablet
but I must write
it is the act of scripturient—
hold instrument in fingers
write until skin cracks and bleeds
when joints swell and burn and ache
until crippled once supple fingers
it is only then
something worth the while comes

There are eons
the muscles in heads only contain so much
eventually, dusty files
collapse in upon themselves
recycled anew for next generations

I was here from the start

the first
and then became
all who'd ever
penned anything
the mind could conceive
recording, reminiscing
tattling, tantalizing
scratching dreams in the dust with bloody finger marks
incanting then decanting
tales of love and lust
saddest dirge of mournful wake
or at the very least
we recorded who we were and who we would be.

I Crossed the Pond

I Spoke with Strangers

Strangers -
I spoke with strangers
for a message
and mapped
new routes
they shared
odd accounts
uncharted territories
Strangers -
I asked their help
and traveled
on unfamiliar vessels
on vast unknown oceans
to places I absolutely
was required to go and quickly
though the cost might be my sanity
I went willingly.

Chimneys of Great Britain

Thousands perhaps millions
Chimneys touch the sky
They spear like dirty little fingers
Stabbing at the blue
Sooty particles plume and belch
Not long ago when it was so cold
The ice rained down
Into falsely pristine air
And felt deceptively clean
But the cold is gone now
And my sweat sticks
Down my back and on my forehead
The clouds move quickly
In the bright blue sky
They are unbelievable
Things of dreams
Grass so green it hurts my heart
How strange my blissful loneliness
I walk completely unknown and lost
And know I could disappear forever
Beyond the chimneys
Into the city or into the country.

The Great Unknown

There is unequivocal fear
of the great unknown
but my thrill of magics cast about
are worth each nervous
ounce of discomfort
and I would not
miss a moment
of this sheer terror
just to be at ease.

Forgiveness, River

River -
I find you
and the spirits too
who walked your banks
and fished and lived
they and we
sat quietly
contemplating
failure and triumph
life unto death
and all of it between.

River -
I love you - I honor you
and those who reside
within and without
please, never fear.

River -
can you find my secrets
many and many
please, keep them close
no one but you may see
into my deepest soul
and may I see
into your currents filled
fortune and sadness.

I will grant you,
will you grant me -
forgiveness, River.

If You Love Me

If you love me
then love me, please
with whatever it is
you have in you.

Whatever it is
I have in me,
is what I will give to you.

But when we're done, my love
then what?

Maybe we'll never be finished
But will run
hands over hearts
and chase eternity
together.

Old Souls

My heart is cherished
by a bevy of old souls
these relative specters
they love me
I amuse them
with my petty machinations
my inane struggle for control.

They were once
such as I am
and remember failings and misdeeds
sadness and small sorrows
being human as they once were
they recognize in me
their own misfortunes
and empathize dearly
but will
never issue warning.

All part of the great mystery
of life and love
being in and of this world
it cannot
and should not
be avoided.

Squirrel King

Hail and well-met, Squirrel King
lovely and plump, you are
with your gamin's glare
you eat your breakfast
quick and dainty
never taking eyes from me
lest I steal
what you believe
belongs within your clutches
never fear, sir
I do not want your seeds and nuts
just a photo, if you please
a moment passed as I
readied to catch
his royal portrait
but him the king
the cute, the scamp -
did not agree
and off he ran
Hail to you, Squirrel King.

Signposts

Signposts
mark our way
my blue day, you do
care about me, that is
and I, you

Saw fate and foible
no need for perfection
it was beautiful
there you were

Clues left in your wake
signposts
a reminder to breathe
and to be kind

It was trust
which I do
these ways with gentle care
in that way of you

What is it that has me
asking perfect strangers
for help
reassuring me

Telling me
it's good
all okay
And blues are just what we do

Because we are gentle souls
looking for inklings

in the signposts
along the way.

Words in Mouth

Words in mouth
and I swallow the ones
I need most.

Whispered across water
in this very real place
the birth of all I hold dear
happened in this spot.

Do not dare abandon me
and drink like sweet wine
all the good ones
I plan to use.

How I deign compare
mine with yours
rattles in my head -
will my arrogance
go unnoticed
rewarded or punished
I would not abase myself
nor be braggart,
as my papa warned me.

What could you possibly need them for now
old man, old Bard
bone and ash and soil
in your time, you spent them all.

Gods, I want it to be my turn
and I'll beg for my chance
but I am terrified
to wake the beast from slumber.

No, I will not beg
I will take.

Please.

I Am Stardust

There are coffins
a few filled with glad hearts
but I have begged
leave mine empty
do not resign
these bones
to the ground
seems a woeful
terrible, waste of space

When I go,
let me go
like a firecracker
cherry bombs
oh, Roman candle
a thousand sparklers
and whistling Pete's
exploding wildly into the night
let it reflect the life I led
and let me return to the stardust I am destined to be.

The Wild Thing

I am
a wild thing
and my thoughts
go to not quite proper.

Listen to me
I've got ideas
and they're not usual,
nor are they tame.

Would it surprise you to know
I am a conundrum even to myself
- how strange -
what is this needy feeling in me
that churns in my soul.

What is this craving for the world
a yearning for whatever else
might be out there
and a desire to meet it.

Discover the new
to find myself
and be amazed
by what I find.

Shakespeare's Garden

I heeded his alluring siren song
from the grave—no need to understand why
traveled dazed and wobbly to this magical place
planted myself on the River Avon banks

Little boats moored at the dock
antiqued and named for romances' sake
Ophelia, Titania, and weeping Juliet
awaited lovers and wandering souls

Even now, none would deny it is his country
imbued with the wild stuff of dreams
every step you sink into his footprint
such hubris—to believe him here with me

Four centuries and more since his death
- but his spirit, I tell you, it lingers
kisses pressed and cries of passion
our pilgrim who waits and watches still

I woke early the morning I was to depart
to tithe my soul at his grave
to meet him and make him love me somehow
Holy Trinity welcomed with open arms

Silently through rows of headstones so old
pavements cracked and pushed asunder
by roots of trees—lichen, leaves, and flowers
in singing distance, water's body flows

I waited while pigeons and swans
sparrows, buntings, and warblers acquiesced

there were locks on gates I dared not enter
and accepted my fate, I could not find him

I saw so much else in missing the man
something strange in his very own garden
how his work transcends blending old with
upstarts like me—I found bliss in the shade of his wealth.

Flights of Fancy

Concerning Pixies

The other day
when we were both younger
you went on and on
about pixies
        where they might hide
        where they might be.

And I thought to myself
it is so fitting
for me to love a man
who speaks with much
seriousness
of mythical beings
that may or may not reside
        in our garden
        in mountainsides
        in cracks between worlds.

I felt a bit envious
that your pragmatic soul
thought of pixies
in the way that you do
and I with my
        soul who wanders
        soul who pines for worlds other than my own
should be the one
most grounded in reality.

But I would never
wish away
your delight in these tiny dreams
        these little bites of magic
        these snippets of sorcery.

My hope for you
is pixies all the way
until it is time for you to travel
your last long journey
and that they wait for you.

Chalice and Knightly Code

A beautiful young man
came to be in my care
his sightless eyes
filled with nightmares
from his days in the wars

He cried out in dreams
and I held up a chalice
to his poor dry lips
and did what I could
to quench his thirst
as he raved in the night

A week went by
and maybe another
by now, the poor boy
was mostly done in

No matter how he ran
his enemy followed
through the battle in his mind
where blood and sweat mingled
on his brave noble brow

On his last day in life
he bowed his head in reverence
drank deeply, then he prayed
he'd upheld his knightly code
and gave thanks to his god

I left him no more than a moment
to gather clean rags
to sop the sweat from his neck

I cried when I found him
my beautiful young man
he died in the night
all alone.

Emblazoned Favors

What is this chivalry?
Sought, emblazoned
upon our memories.

I am so taken
so fascinated
by lore
of pilgrimages and feasts
and tournaments
but more and vital
real acts of bravery
no mere sporting event.

And do I drop
my favor?
Never!

I'd rather be
member of the guard
in the charge
the muck and mire and blood
as the clash of steel on steel
rings in my ears
and my certain death
is nigh
and honor restored
to my family home.

Or strange witch in a cave
revered for compassion
timely works wrought
or wrathful might
when wrong is done

to those much weaker -
the lonely life
is not so alone
when budding
acolyte appears
in the mist.

But to be
only chattel
or even chatelaine
a daughter, a wife
a mother, a crone
dead before born
learn stitches precisely
be at mercy
of years and time and men
of childbirth and being born a woman -
the strongest survive.

The Cussing Monk

They awaken me
before I've rested
then my patience
truly tested
terrible mattress
worst haircut
uncomfortable bench
to place my butt
the tallow in these candles
stinks to high heaven
when the brothers sing
turn it to eleven
but I've got a secret
and no one else knows
I'm a woman in
a monk's clothes.

Desolate Wilderness of the Mind

He crawled for weeks
amidst a desolate wilderness
his mind ablaze and afraid
heart weary
searching thoughts
strings of ideas
was he not due a trip profound
encased by bounty of pleasure
and just at the moment
he would have given up all hope
there he found a room
a memory palace
filled to overflowing
scented by the idea of her
her secrets, her powers
no small measures, only tranquility
and he wondered how it was
she could find her way
on this scattered path
with such apparent ease
when all the while he suffered so.

What exactly did she do differently
and would she be willing to share her gifts?

Nightmare Carousel

I rode that night
on the darkened carousel
made from the broken
lost objects
things no one wanted
sadness and sighs
those filled with madness
toothless, crying tigers
red-eyed ostriches
with poisoned wings
the sharpened claws
of salivating ponies
their stamping hooves
cutting into the boards
so close to me.

I was ringmaster of the carnival
how tables had turned
until I became the beast
and awaited liberation
pulling at iron bars
to no avail.

And then I awoke in a sweat
nightmares faded slowly, into the dawn.

Submitted for Your Inspection
- a mystery poem

There were myths
and misdirection
although everything was denied
the mystery seem unsolvable
quirks of case had been implied.

Or was it pre-ordained
this propensity
for officers of the day
to cry out, "insanity"
as they stood and watched
the madness in the rain.

They squandered
time and motivation -
what they lacked, it was intensity -
the insurrection's coming
all were sure it was calamity.

Regardless of their claims
this case of mistaken identity
led all to believe - answer must be
coordination at the gallery.

Come to find the answer's clear
a painting had gone missing -
they scratched their heads
gave loads of thought
who is to blame
what should be done.

One charmless guard,
a harried wife,

the delivery driver,
two teenage girls.

Do you know?
And can you guess?
This submitted for your
inspection.

Left to Ashes

Dinner was over
in the quiet house
Midcentury Modern
echoes
heels tap
at linoleum floors
fingers tap
at wood paneled walls
hands wipe oiled soap
so carefully
take care of it, dear
and it will take care of you
only it didn't -

Fireplace left to ashes
close the sheers and the drapes
arrange the flowers
in heavy vases
she wondered
could she make herself stop
preparing meals
for absent love
extinguished dreams
broken promises -
stacked plates
leftovers into the freezer
napkins refolded -
maybe tomorrow, not today.

Sat on the Curb

The past is a faded photo
of warnings and roadmaps and star-charts
race with me to the back of beyond
where we'll find the markers

be brave
I really need you
to be brave

I sat on the curb
and waited for you to come home
hoped and dreamed
for things I didn't dare ask

be brave
I really need
to be brave

let the dust kick up a storm
emotion whirlwind
particles float on breezes
sucked into the vortex we created
when we created
this matrix and maelstrom

be brave
I think
I can be brave

—sometimes these things
come out nonsense of a madwoman
and we have to be satisfied
there's anything at all to be mined

other times it's
all purity and righteous verse
so I'll just leave this here
to ponder
I'll wait an eternity—

be brave
we're gonna
be brave

I sat on the curb
dust on my knees, grease on my chin
and waited for you to come home.

Transient Dreams

I think it might be like this.

Thoughts speed by
but we move through time at snail's pace.
We believe we are on top of things, in charge
and the boss of it all -

Instead,
we lope along
one life experience
to the next
and we watch
as they become
transient dreams.

We wait,
our every step
oozing indolence
yet inside our minds
roil with excitement
and dread
and wonderment.

There might be
anything trying to
skitter or slide
down dusty corridors.
And we pine to see
what we might.

We open a door here
window cracked there
slam it shut on the other side

and feel rusty edges of dirty hinges.

Sounds brush up
against the backs of our necks.
Gaze — watery reflections
watch them shift, ripple
according to
sunshine, rainfall, moonrise
and the shadows of clouds cast
as they careened over mountaintops -
could not guess
how fast they moved.

We watched while weeping
at how they played hide and seek
with certain lightness as it caressed the land.
      it feels like chance
      strange coincidence
      preponderance of resource.
Blithely unaware,
the world beyond -
merely an idea,
solitary and selfish
and we are itinerant specters moving
one railway yard to the next
relying on the kindness of strangers.

Memento Mori

Puccini's Tables

I used to love a little place
once upon a time
on Columbus Avenue
I'd turn up when I could
just to feel alive and whole.

I'd grab a corner seat
watch foot traffic
as crowds milled about
sometimes the owner greeted
always a surprise
city of eight hundred thousand
I wasn't quite a local, not a tourist either
mid-distance I supposed
in a hierarchy of caffeine.

I watched in fascination
old-timers as they gathered
reminiscing and then sipping
doppio espresso with a twist
lemon on the side -
I tried to be part of their pack
with a hunk of raw sugar
just at the edge of my spoon
and sucked my drink through it
like I was someone special, somewhere.

The namesake was Puccini
they played opera for the masses
over tired stereo speakers
homemade cannoli and minestrone
I cannot lie, it was divine.

It burned down years ago
I cried when I thought of all my visits
my mom, my cousin, my daughter, my husband
and so many, many friends
I loved that little cafe
my time outside of time
I'll never forget the pleasure I had
when I sat at Puccini's tables.

Deluxe Between the Lines

Sometimes
Root beer
There were inklings
Aqua Velva
Of who you were
Hair grease
Then before I knew it
Deluxe burgers
You'd close the door tight
Drill press
What happened, Daddy
Thick-rimmed glasses
I didn't really know you
Motorcycles
And then
Garage
You were gone.

Old Woman

For years I watched an old woman
as she walked along the oceanfront
choosing bits of shells and driftwood
and hid them softly in pockets deep
each day like a prayer, she practiced
and saved those things
that mattered not to others.

I wondered who would save her
as I watched her daily catechism
and finally realized maybe saving
wasn't at all what she wanted
perhaps she needed a friend to abide
her lonely ramble across the sand
and to carefully climb the rocks
with sure and certain footing.

I thought I should join her
and give her flowers from my garden
thinking she'd add them to the treasures
she so lovingly cared for
I would be her friend, and we would talk
of matters most important.

One day when the morning light
came crisply through my window
I raced through my routine
so I wouldn't miss her amble
I gathered my flowers and fixed my smile
the sun was a lovely shade of happiness
and the windswept breeze
mussed my hair in all directions
but she never showed

and I never saw her again in this life.

For years I wondered what happened to her
why didn't she come back?
where had she gone?
I took up the mantle, collecting those shells
and walked the lonely shores
I watched a young woman, who in turn was watching me
my life had come full circle, becoming a mirror
forward and backward in time
I smiled to myself, satisfied to know
one day, she would bring me flowers.

Winding Time

Dutch wall clock
reminds us finally
winds the days away
to you
no longer with us
every 48 hours
this pretty metronome
a rhythm of life passing
weights
must be pulled
otherwise, it stops
and then you're to advance
the time as though
magician and traveler

I hear his voice
you know
his accent and love
I miss your dad
and the strong echoes
of his life

Always to the right
never to the left
if you don't go
in proper direction
it won't work
might break
then where will you be
cannot go backward
when dealing with time
no matter how you might wish
when time's done, it's done

And while you're at it, son,
keep it dusted
lovingly and often
keep the gears
from gumming up
this clock from your Oma
came to me and now to you
goodbye
I'd give anything, you know
to be with you once again.

Lost Days and Found

Silent.
We crept
Along precious edges
Of softly moving water.

Sweet clover
Dragonfly
Waterbug shadows.

Here is where the shape
   of this body
Manifested space
By moss-covered rocks
Cattails, and wild iris
Where liquid flows
Heavy as whipping cream
Light and sweet
   in metallic tinkling songs
Or the thrum of a life force clapping.

Look to those and marvel
So careful, drinking fawn,
Always wary
   the dangers of the forest
Fat and pretty rainbow trout
Shimmering under nature's gaze
Found a perfect resting spot
Slumbers in creek's bed
There the miner's lettuce
   and, darling, watercress, too.

Feed yourself well, beauty

   if you know where to look
Sometimes picking wild berries
Plucking time's tender morsels
Placed between the heaven of your lips.

Close my eyes
Imagine
That you were never gone
   and I'd keep you with me
Rays of sun cast beams spearing water droplets
Make fools of us mere mortals
   and sometimes shiny diamonds.

Soliloquy of the Dead

       Will you visit me now that I'm gone?
No sadness, please. Just come say hello.
Maybe bring flowers. I love delphiniums.
Bring a picnic. Stay a while. Tell me all about you.
I'd love to see pictures.
The little ones must be all grown up.
Time is different here.
Oh, you're leaving.
Do you think your friends would like to call on me?
Just a visit, it's so quiet here, and I'm lonely.
I do miss family gatherings.
Right, you must go.
Well, goodbye then.
I love you so.

       Someone's here.
A gentleman caller, for me?
Really?
Oh, it's the gardener—he's nice—but he doesn't talk much.
Used to be folks came quite often. Not anymore.
No family now.
Just strangers. I suppose I don't mind.
Better than nothing.
The teenagers making out is a wee bit much.
And the girls in black lipstick who try to speak with us.
Don't get me wrong, if you wake me, I will speak.
Even if I have no idea who you are.
Did I mention I was lonely?

       Hello! It's really nice to see you.
A séance? I used to love those when I was young.
I've been waiting quite a while.
Are you pleased to see me too?

No, I don't know where the jewelry was hidden.
Or the money or your nana's recipes.
Oh! You think he was murdered? I have no idea.
I don't know anything that can help you.
I'm terribly sorry.
I'm just here, and you're just there.
Goodbye.

    Hello? Hello? Please, will you speak with me?
All I want is the news of the world I once inhabited.
How is that lady? How are her children?
No, I can't remember their names.
Do you know my family? Do you know who I am?
It seems as though I used to know.
But my mind's become quite blank.

    Wait, don't leave, please don't go.
Maybe I can help you.
I've been dying for company.
People come here to see the crying lady spirit.
Is that me?
Do I cry overly much?

Her Soul's Journey

Mourning evaporates into mist
lock front door one last time
the longest journey she'd begun
to find her kith and kin

curiosity - what might happen
in this newest now
she looked back to sleep and shadows
no longer feeling bones and marrow

nothing left of her to hold
as things once were, she cannot have
no petty time for matter and meaning
only forward can she go

no one left to recognize
looks upon them now as strangers
stops and wonders how far she's come
and shakes her head, it doesn't clock

whispers - melancholy descends
she searches lone existence
while to the left and to the right
odd specters drawing nigh

confusion overtaking purpose
trudging further is how it goes
looks behind sadly understanding
she'll never see this place again

further forward path has narrowed
soft lights glow upon horizons
lining pathways as she floats

cherished ones departed decades past

sighs to see those kindly faces
satisfaction's balm replacing worry
embraced by spirits come to welcome
her soul's journey is at sweet end.

Paper Cranes

We strung paper cranes on fishing line
hung them
over bedroom windows
symbolic
        folded by a loved one
        ascended several years prior
the dissonance of cancer enough
you outlived predictions
made your wishes known
you didn't ask for much
it was not our death
but we
behaved in ways
contrary to the norm
self-consciousness evaporated
I read Gatsby to you
made Valentine's Day cards
spoke my peace and my love
inadequacies stifled
reared their ugly heads
while I slept unsoundly
and then
early one morning
you stopped
you were gone by the time I'd arrived
my sister and I sat in near darkness
breathing
speaking in low tones
about what we believed might be true
        all these years gone
        and I still have some of your ashes
        in an old teapot
we saw the fairy lights

up in the corner
and knew your soul hovered
it danced with the paper cranes.

On the Precipice

When I heard the news
I keened
like an animal, I was.
The sounds I made
primal and shredded
ripped from my chest.

Because I could imagine
what it was for you
to stand on that edge
with the wind in your hair
stinging your cheeks
bringing tears to your eyes
and a tremble to your lip.
You dressed in red
from your head to your toes.

Feeling so helpless
out there
precipice of eternity
vibrations from traffic and
someone must have seen you -
gorgeous statuesque glory.

More afraid of living
than you were of dying.
And that last glimpse of torment
god, I would spare you that
spare you everything if I could
but I can't.

And then, darling, you flew.

You are so missed, my friend.

Spells, Dreams, Incantations

I've Drawn Down the Moon

I've drawn down the moon
bathed in her glory
how she chills and warms me
my wishes heard, the pleas
when eventide's darkness
weighs heavy upon me
I gather her close
luminescence casting lights on tides
reflections on sacred waters
mystic plains and valleys
mountains quiver at her incantations
she has mesmerized and
settled over me
her magical cloak
resting gentle on
hips and shoulders
lips and thighs
she protects the sensual night
and fond delights are found
within the glow of her
ever-changing, beautiful face.

Moving Pencils

I sat for hours
and tried to move a pencil
across the table
with my mind.

Presuming I could do magic
or BE magical
probably a side effect of
Stephen King or Mary Stewart
HA! or perhaps
Carlos Castaneda.

It didn't seem to work
but I was a persistent girl, aged 9
precociously well read
just evading
everyday life.

I kept trying to move the pencil
with my mind
across the table -
it wouldn't budge.

Water witches
back in England
father's side
the dowser passed the power
to the men in the family
but why not me?

My great grandfather's spirit
inhabited a formal portrait -
years after his death

he'd move it on the wall
at family gatherings
hello, I am still here.

I began to wonder
if indeed that magic
skipped me altogether
because I was a girl
or perhaps my talents
lie elsewhere.

I could not move that pencil
or find water in the yard
no matter how many pits I dug
I couldn't make it happen
or make my life less chaotic.

I noted though, as years went by
a little miracle here or there
and I felt my powers rise
as a creative human being
finally there was the magic
I sought so hard to find
but I still cannot move pencils.

My Divination

Your divine
ain't so sublime
my divination
procrastination

tarot works
for those who wait
like suckin' jelly
from the marrow

throw the bones
brew the leaves
chants some chants
do as you please

shake, shake mama
magic 8 ball
just as good as
some of the others

I could name
if I could remember
light the candle
cook the book

you never know where
the dice will fall
never know where
pendulum doth rest

yes or no
move the planchette
ouija says

get over it

betwixt, between
it doesn't matter
oracle's got
just one more spell

there's those who know
and those who don't
then those who'd steal
and cause you pain

no disrespect
meant for those who truly see
I only mean to chide
the ones who'd harm the weak

let it be a lesson
or a warning
whatever you might need
do no harm to me and mine

lest it come back upon you
three times divine.

Clairvoyant's Bend

Go to
the river
where the
berry is red
and stone
circles round
sip water
from moss
take to the hills
before you weep
those who will
you'll know in your mind
those who wait
beyond the veil
they know
the past
you'll say
what comes
clairvoyant's bend
will see you done.

Grind

Take gristle and bone
now, grind it fine
When you think it's done
you do it again
Deep in the marrow
deep in the cuts
Grind it together
with mortar and pestle
Circle the fire
thrice and then
Circle you back
again, again.

I Don't Shy Away

I am no babe in the woods
when it comes to mystical
a world between worlds
magic beyond the veil
or deep inside the looking glass.

I gave myself permission
to follow the trail
my own imagination - unlimited.

The whispers didn't leave
when I grew up
talk of certain family members
on either side
it came to be
through my blood and bones
before I was starlight manifest
were generations of the wise.

Spells and rituals
altars and incantations
all were mine
and the gifts
sometimes frightened
but I never shied away.

I wield small but kind power
answers from ancestors
dreams that have two meanings
esoteric itch between my shoulders
that cold chill of knowing
and poems
they are my invocations.

Making Memory Work

Gaze
these light patterns
relax
let spirit soar
breaths come slow and deep
as I come closer to the veil
to speak with those who might
give audience.

Open conduit
viable channel
frisson and electricity
love becomes energy
wake up sleeping beings
I wish to speak with you.

I have spoken with departed
those whose
chapters have run out
sometimes
they desire
to impart last wisdom
boons concluding
closing sonnets
burning questions
of love's last gleaming
and I will aid them
to the last of my breath.

My soul has a contract signed
generations before I was born
to archive, collect, impart
familial wisdom

and right those things
which are wrong
their deeds meld fast
deep in my memory
connection shared unbreakable
and lest you think
I've acquired indentured debt
to the cause
I have
my servitude lasts lifetimes
without end
and is the best most beautiful work
I've ever done.

Light Worker Ways

Light works its way into darkness
it scratches and digs
transforming fear into hope
first scent perhaps decay
second is herb as it blends
what is it now?
well trodden wood
gleams with oil
long before it splinters into dirt
and begin its life in the circle again.

Chilled stone and cold hearth
only a small bit of what is needed for warmth
sweep those motes
prepare to begin
this place of worship
not comforted by dank
or scant cleanliness
light works—will always work its way through darkness.

Gather belongings and songs and psalms
know it rote, know it best
this ancient birth
what origins to be believed
words pass over lips and into being -

Spell me a moment,
let me rest
spill the words,
off my chest
sing the spell,
truly blessed.

They leave their vessel
not cast out
but mingle gently
with four winds
gathering power, gathering reality
light works its way
out of darkness.

Seanchaí to the Spirits

Walking truth
through my forest darkly
illuminating full moon
snow-filled berms
safe passage phantasm
I approach the meeting place
a site out of shadows
where night sky looks down
stars gently watch
and wait for magic to bloom
the scent of snow
and pine
mixed with curiosity
I wait until
her presence is felt
at my shoulder
my angel, my mother
my silent conduit to the past
patiently
they gather
form an unbreakable circle
generations filling spaces
my ancestors
I hear their breathing
hearts beating
feel movements
and approval
a gospel of utter stillness
while thoughts flow freely
into and out of my mind
each spirit has come
of their own accord
to see the next *seanchaí*

take a spot in history
just one nod
and I am theirs.

Music Memory

David Bowie

God, I miss David Bowie
His music, my coming of age
Grew up with him
He meant something - means something

Cheryl's sister's 45s
Fame and Golden Years
Writing down lyrics
In that painstaking way we had back then

In darkness in bed at night - memorizing
Singing quietly under cover
For all the things in life that weren't right
David Bowie was very much right

Maybe in alternate timelines
Ziggy's in
Another galaxy
He's doing his thing
God, I hope
He's doing his thing

In his honor - for his honor
Look up here; he's in Heaven
Everybody knows him
And I painted something

Called it
The Beloved
Because for me, he is
And not just me -

That painting
I didn't know
What I was doing
Or how to execute
It wasn't good; I did not care
Only had to make something
Lasting, just because

Now, I see it when I pass
From the corner of my eye
Or when
I look straight on - clouds and sky and heart

I think of him
How he made me feel
When I was young
Invincible comes to mind
Strange and lovely, too.

Transistor Sister Radio

Seventh birthday
caught the flu
pneumonia hit and party cancelled
sick and feverish I was bereft
so hard to remember much except
darkened bedroom
sweating, shivering, listening
favorite present
transistor sister radio
with the tiny little speaker
I could listen along
KYA or KFRC songs
up to my ear
and hear
yesterday and today
> *a thumb goes up, a car goes by*
> *so, bye, bye Miss American Pie*

so much life already stored
banking memories
> *good times never seemed so good*
> *been all around the world*

in my mind
I've got all those old songs
and all of the dreams
> *hold me darling just a little while*

transistor sister radio.

Hitchin' a Ride - Vanity Fare
American Pie - Don McLean
Brand New Key - Melanie
Sweet Caroline - Neil Diamond
Last Kiss - J Frank Wilson and the Cavaliers

Bad Brains

Bad news, bad tidings
no comfort, no joy
stuck inside
she can't deny

bad brains
anachronistic
tendencies
fails the same
the chemistry is suspect
put her on a train
wants to be a rebel
tries to rebel

bad brains, bad brains
the bane of her existence
what a strain
like a stain down the drain
the accusations are insane
in the membrane

bad brains, bad brains
who the fuck knows
she doesn't know
she only knows she wants

bad brains
can't seem to
understand
they don't
understand

bad brains, bad brains

punk scene
kills frustrations
makes more punks
bad brains.

1970s Speakers

Stereo trying
to keep up
with my demand
not modern
conveniences
just increase
the volume
bass and treble
and pray
I didn't blow
my speakers
convinced The Clash
could hear my
scream-shouts
an ocean away.

Headphones
all night long
stack those LPs
pray
for no skips
those were
my lullabies
wake early
hear that
scratching
dissonance
needle stuck
at the end
of the last song.

One more
before school

better make it
a good one
get the heart
bumping
make the blood flow
Mom's yelling
"Breakfast"
in the kitchen
down below
just increase
the volume
and pray
I didn't blow out my ears.

Patti Smith's Words

I am smitten with
Patti Smith's words
transfixed.

Sure I'd see her in New York
walking down the street
her cool self meeting
awkward me
maybe on the beach
maybe on the subway
maybe at a restaurant
gallery, museum, bar, a park
I am smitten with
Patti Smith's words.

I didn't see her
I didn't meet her
but I felt her presence
in a bookstore
a lovely place
beautiful and used
crowded poems and pulp
filled with paper
that changed lives
recounted dreams
sang praises
opened minds
tears to eyes
I am smitten with
Patti Smith's words.

There are souls
who understand

and there are souls who don't
call me whatever you want to call me
but her words are written
invisible ink on my skin
not so mad, I just want to be blessed
like prayers and benediction
I am smitten with
Patti Smith's words.

Stella by Starlight

What would it be
to see her there
lights cast
light fast
her steps in darkness
illuminated
gentle thoughts
and starlight

softly whispered sighs
a touch, a glance
pining for her
the way he did
when the world
was younger
than it will ever be again
by starlight

lips move
silky slow
purposeful intent
her pulse
the corner of her mouth
indrawn breath
ecstatic moment
she is starlight.

Necessity: Come Worship at the Altar of the Eccentric

Divine mother of invention
holy Aphrodite's oil
'tis necessity
she opened her mouth and yelled
then she shouted
hey!
might we be
reaching nirvana tonight
and she hooted, she hooted
like a *nite* owl swooping over
showing up at Joe's garage
no LSD just revelry
when she saw what she had wrought
dig this wild man - this freak, Frank
brilliant in his guise
no disguise - never him -
who he was and ever shall be
and I made him - she crowed
him,
dripping with relevant irreverence
iconic polymath
polymorphic tendencies
meditations and preparations
brethren waited with bated breaths
come with me babies on the Inca Road
ah yeah, and bring your peaches
we're going - city of tiny *lites*
and the girls in the neighborhood say
no, no, no
don't waste your time
git you the pancake breakfast

doesn't he just make you go, WOW!

My many thanks and gratitude to Frank Zappa
I sampled words and inspiration from the following:
Inca Roads
Joe's Garage
Peaches En Regalia
City of Tiny Lites
Cosmik Debris
St. Alfonzo's Pancake Breakfast

True Love's Kiss

Are You There?

Dear you.
It's some time
since I've wanted to trust
my heart stuff here.

But the universe is shaking my bones,
speaking in ways I cannot misunderstand
and I must take a moment to impart
the love that is in my heart, stranger
simply because we exist
in this world - at this time.

I hope to my depths
that this finds you
well and feeling comforted -
can you feel the touch
as I reach out my hand,
your skin against mine,
if only as is imagined
in this vast cosmic place,
the caring we all
so very much need.

I will exhale in relief
when I know you are
all right and that
we are still
in this world together
at the same time
just holding on.

Because we are made up of
connections large and small

we might never have been aware
of the ripple that is another's existence.

I don't need to know you
to understand
with my whole heart
you're importance to me
I am grateful for you -
we are not alone in this universe.

He Manifests

He manifests -
I watch astounded
by his alacrity -
how he manipulates
those swirling elements
in heavy air -
thick oppressive
with humid intentions
of summer afternoons
I wonder, slightly worried
what was it he asked for

He manifests -
things seemingly
of no consequence
his eloquence
a secret language
only he seems
to understand
just destiny
and dreams
they race to finish
those dispossessed
let it be the acid test
it was no accident
depression following
broken heart

He manifests -
took his time
to heal, to learn
melancholia
addressed

trace evidence
examined with
fine-toothed comb
he drew those things
he needed most
close to his center
I wanted
desperately to be
that which he needed

He manifests -
brought them
into existence
barely seeing
dynamism
mojo's reason
a golem altar
to his will
he may have joked
but it was known
he did invoke
his power thresholds
ebb and flow
acceptance was elusive
as he straddled the moving lines
co-mingled
disbelief and understanding.

A Dream for the Young and Inclined

We met at a party
when I was very young
and he asked me to dance.
*Sway with me
under the moonlight -*
he whispered in my ear.

A pretty excuse
to get close
while music played
and meteors fell to earth.

Later he took me home
on the back of his bike
And I knew it then
there was something
real waiting for me -
so, I reached out to him
and held on tight.

He showed up
one morning
on my porch, hat in hand
asked me so sweet -
*Walk along with me
down old dirt roads.
Come walk with me
we'll go for a while
watch the trestle for trains
smell the oil and diesel
and pick wildflowers.
Be my come and go, girl -
You know there's nowhere*

I'd rather be.

I fell in love with a boy
and he fell in love with me
and begged me
to give him half a chance.
*Darlin' if you'd be
so inclined.*

He told me
he'd love me forever
and I said I would, too.
We made our lives
so magic, so sweet together
in one another's arms.

Spaces Between Us

Sometimes
in the kitchen
when I look at you
I cannot figure out
how we got to this place -
I try to trace it all back
to the beginning.

There is a softness about us, now
a kindness, an enduring patience
there is also vexation.

A tiny rock in the shoe
that won't come out
each step taken
shifts the pebble
makes itself known
in myriad ways
I keep walking on it
knowing the damn thing
won't move
until it's good and ready.

All emotions
crash down at once
I gasp as truth hits me
squarely in the chest
you are my growing up
and my growing old
and all of the years in between
I'd be lying
if I didn't say
the spaces that have appeared
sometimes hurt my heart.

The Pleasure of Your Company

There is such grace
in your smile
the sound of your laughter
some little thing
you share with me
stories and moments
your songs, your opinions
the pleasure of you
can sometimes be
blessing, curse
surprise
and conundrum.

You are a prayer
in an existence
I sometimes
have trouble
believing.

It washes over me
as you exasperate
more I am sure,
than another
human being
in the history
of human beings
possibly could -
I wouldn't trade us
for anything in this universe
or the next
and there is such grace in your smile.

To the River

Come down with me to the river
I'll show you my peace and salvation
Meet me there when the sun is high
Collect ferns and play skipping stones
Egrets will spy from high above
And marvel when troops of ants march.

I've gone to the river to cleanse my soul
The thing in my life that makes sense
Soft light of morning, it beckons me
Moon and sun claim faintly. and I wonder
What will I be when all's said and done
And disappear within this blissful revelry.

Cross the river, and please find me
Miracles - be there as sun sinks so low
And sky turns a magical pink
Tell me your secrets - I'll tell you mine
Sink your toes into the warm muddy silt
And feel that satiny ooze divine.

Join me, love, on the banks of the river
I'll wait 'til the moon casts silvery light
Across ripples that touch and claim magic
On the shores of an alchemical body
Float troubles downstream 'til they disappear
Humbled and thankful - begging nature's rendezvous.

Heart, Soul, and Mind

Eager Mornings

I am not eager in mornings
to greet the dawn
to greet the day
instead, I shuffle to the kitchen, head down
hair askew - a wild design
pour coffee, with cream, *slurp*
no conversation yet
too soon, too soon.

You are outside
binoculars at eyes
earnestly watching the sky
for our neighbors the raptors
or errant puffs of smoke
to spy fire planes
and listen to the
brrapp, brrapp, brrapp
motorcycle sounds
on the highway
in the distance
rooster crows.

We sit and stare out
our voices low
trading ideas, observances
things we've never said before
things we say often.

It's going to be hot
over a hundred today
we will sweat
sun will try to fry us
like eggs on cement, *sizzle*

but right now
there is peace
birds splash in bath
and chat at the feeder
dog suspiciously charming.

Aging

I miss the places I can never go again
the chances I took and the ones I missed
I'm only this way once, and then I'm gone
I'll travel on to those furthest shores
there are moments - I get moments
a perfect peach, a delicate wing
do you get them, too - I have such hope
do not squander - for they are glorious

I miss the younger woman I was
standing in afternoon's brilliant sun
with my fancy cowboy boots on
wave to the world for dear life
laughter comes with tears in eyes
a younger work-in-progress
and I didn't know who I'd be
it was still around the corner

I miss the older woman I'll be
toes in the sand, holding hands
with my uncertain future
and look back at silly young miss
eyes full of love and promise
I'll know the stories of what I've done
maybe forgetting everything that I've known
I'll walk my miles 'til I reach home.

Defiance

I kept my defiance
locked up tight
but it was present
in every breath
and each beat
of my secret heart.
My words
were flags waving in the wind
against
hard and soft targets -
they spoke of
human heartache
vulnerability
kindness and love.

I cannot, will not stop.

Rebellious Heart

I am no insurrectionist
nor am I riotous, alienating, seditious
but the word rebellious
it sets my heart on fire.

Maybe there's something wrong
that a word such as this
would make my juices flow
or that my eyes would sparkle
like the light of a thousand flames.

Think of me, please, and tell me
am I—difficult, unruly, turbulent?
is defiant
not too far from the mark?

My freedom
will never be passively granted
there must be toil, it must be earned
with blood from my veins day after day.

I believe I equate it with
wild mustangs
galloping, thundering hooves, flowing manes
these horses serve as a reminder to me
what my soul aches for
what I crave.

Skitter

The word
feels sinister
a semblance of presentiment
I relish the sound as it sits
in my mouth, my mind
sibilant but not serpentine
sinuous grace, perhaps, no
which implies certain
lack of finesse or poise
but still
it moves at speed with alacrity
consider the lizard
as it makes its way
across a hard-packed desert
dog-claws
in need of a trim
on the hardwood floor
dry autumn leaves
scratching against each other
over the front sidewalk
and the skitter of black widow
as she builds a silent trap.

Whim

I have
done
strange
things
at the drop of a hat
that you couldn't quite imagine
odd
seems to be
my stock in trade
and I've made mistakes
aplenty
I cannot regret
a thing I recall -
to exist on a whim
is freedom for
heart and soul and everything.

Wine Glass

I drink wine
from a glass
of no consequence.
To be honest,
I've consumed it
out of
a coffee mug
beer glass
Scooby-doo jelly jar
and please don't repeat
but I have sucked it
delightfully
straight from
the bottle.
I own many wine glasses
and it is strange to me
no matter
which I purchase
they never feel right
in size or shape
I've certainly
smashed my fair share.
I know I could solve
my mystery of wine glasses
if I really cared
but after all, it is not the vessel
it is the drink.

Golden Opportunities

What is this thing
dwelling dormant within me?
I was the same person
my entire life
waiting for
the unnameable
a golden opportunity
but never
grasping
that brass ring
others seemed so sure of.

One morning
I woke up, aware
there were differences
in the way
I felt about myself.

An unfamiliar scent on the wind
the leaves on the trees seemed
more determined, stronger
resilient and beautiful
colors more vivid
dripping with flavor
perception sharp and canny
I felt...

Is it merely me
a transient wanderer
hitchhiker
with thumb out
backpack over shoulder
or

will I settle in and settle down -
for the long haul?
I am honest
when I say
I could not guess.

Only that I'm curious and waiting
to see what happens next.

Infatuated Girl

I am a curious girl
infatuated by
nine thousand
eight hundred
sixty-seven
things a day -
ideas and ways
people and books
plants and rocks and bugs.

I fall in love so easily
most times without grace
just *bam*, and I'm there.

My brain doesn't recognize
a slow build -
only a total and instant
commitment -
to the thing wiggling under
my microscope
oldies songs on the radio
the bread in my basket
a bird at the feeder
or a delicate laugh
and always
childlike wonderment for rainbows.

My eye perceives
my heart beats
and there I am
infatuated
by nearly everything new
that comes my way.

The Knell of Electric Death

The cord is frayed
and look at the socket
it's patched
with narrow black tape
left over from times
that no longer exist
and people long dead
it's making connections
with devices long since
past their prime.

When you turn on the hair dryer
there shouldn't be sparks -
what exactly is going on inside
the walls of this old house
you know, my darling
that's how fires start.

I wonder absently
how many sessions remain
before the damn thing blows
a sure sign of being grown up
you find yourself
at Ace Hardware
making purchases
early on Saturday morning
it was never mentioned
you'd have to attend
to matters such as these.

I remember my papa's house
before it was mine
the fuse box hidden

downstairs in the cloak closet
with his tidy pencil scratchings
on a perfect peeling label
a treasure map
for the clueless
who try to guess
which one was blown
with crossed fingers and breaths held
and relief when presumption is right
we escape the knell of electric death.

Finding Balance

There will always be
the fear that I must
give away the parts of me
that I am meant to keep
otherwise you will not like me
you will tell me I am not worthy
or deserving of your time
it doesn't matter
that this isn't true
or that it might be -

Silly as it may seem
it's the first place I wander
I see how skewed
are the words on the page
it is then I know
my program's a little broken
what lives in my brain
and dines on my soul
just a bit of not right -

This time I think
I'll try something new
a balance if you will
where I can still love and be loved
can still show up
without fear of emptying my cup
and thirsting to death
with no drop left
because I am worthy
I deserve this balance.

Out of Dog Food

Wake up
 make coffee
 begin a new day
 coffee drips
 I'm impatient with the little details of my life
 told it would be fast—the coffee—it isn't that fast
 stare at today
 lacking motivation
 as I sometimes am
 and that will not do
 it makes for boring words
 or rather—dull choices
 let us not blame the English language
 for my moods, I decide
 it's grey, rain forecasted
 Summer's gone, I suppose
 this is my best time of year
 most favorite
 and the worst, the hardest
 for me
 always.

Wake up
 sit at desk
 think of writing
 write
 edit
 not just any piece
 but this piece, here
 the one you're reading
 has already morphed
 quite a few times
 I'll decide which will make the cut.

Wake up
 wait for coffee
 why make myself wait?
 it's a game I play
 just to let me know I'm in control of any little thing in my life
 stirring in the other room—hello, you.

Wake up
 coffee time
 feed dog.

Wake up
 laugh about groundhogs
 pay bills
 bemoan state of finances.

Wake up
 happy to be alive
 it's how it starts
 how it ends
 and finally, how it goes
 predestined, or so they say
 those believers in such things
 I say it's my life
 then I wonder
 I make it up as I go along, you know—how's that working for me?

Wake up
 wait for the coffee to stop dripping
 out of milk
 and dog food
 run to the store
 this day begins in irritation
 and I will do nearly anything
 to avoid that
 and yet
 I still run out of milk

still run out of dog food
because I'm not perfect.

Wake up.

Wolf Thanksgiving

One year
my family of three
escaped the mayhem
of the city
for Thanksgiving in the mountains.

A blanket of fresh snow
greeted us the next morning
clear and bright - a bluebird sky
and ice crystals shone like diamonds
in late-autumn sun
we needed milk for breakfast
so bundled up tight for a walk
to the general store on the highway
a pristine day - but cold, so cold
it brooked no argument
about scarves
boots, gloves, and hats.

The silence was sacred
broken only
by our breaths
and the crunching of our boots
on the snow's icy crust
we made fresh tracks
and celebrated the dearth of society
as peace enveloped
the mostly empty cabins with few wisps of smoke
from chimneys here and there.

Off in the distance
a large dog skulked along - hunched
he was graceful and loping

clocking our scent and movement
he kept us in view
let us come a little closer
and to our astonishment
not a dog
nor coyote
but a wolf
in an area where wolves hadn't existed
in gods only knew how long.

The closer we came to him
the more enormous his truth became
perhaps a dream
we wondered -
were we to be joined
by brother wolf?

He traveled with us together
a momentary pack
but he disappeared
when the sounds of the highway encroached
and we knew
we'd experienced true magic.

The Sorry State of Utility

If you saw my hands
you'd know they are
instruments of busy
not beauty, grace, or winsomeness.

I bemoaned the sorry state
of my appendages
to my mother
when I was still a child -
I had yet to gain
wrinkles or unsightly creases
or fucking age spots, burns, and scars -
she laughed and said
my hands were industrious
it was her way of
trying to make me feel better
which it emphatically did not
all I saw was ugly and uninteresting utility.

But now I see
lives built
ideas wrought
hands held
cheeks cradled
tears shed and then lovingly wiped away.

These hands hold on to dear life.

Highways of Kindness

I think about kindness
all of the time.

What I believe -
it's an inexhaustible engine
but the pump needs to be primed
the tank filled
and in exchange
if guarded ever so carefully
it becomes
a never-ending resource.

All that is required - the essential bit -
is that we begin
with a selfless act which is the fuel
to start down this self-perpetuating
journey of grace
as it is set in motion.

The more of us on the road the better
and anyone can join -
perfection not required -
sincerity a must.

Here is the time for all lanes full
absolutely gridlocked
and my dream becomes reality.

Every Sort of Midnight

Absolute midnight
where magic and mayhem dwell
moves with gentle frailty
careful and quiet motions
of last story ideas
a verse waiting to be born
and cannot decide
whether to approach
on a Wednesday or a Thursday
when all else slumbers fast.

Tears held at bay choose now
practically midnight
the fevered, the confused
sad reveries flourish in this soft time
these whispered plans
and lingering touches
grateful palms
meeting palms
or lips or cheeks.

Eyes spy clock
counting down
time wants and you
believe there's more
where that came from
how can it be
molasses
fleeting
un-waiting
short
the midnight hour lies
says you'll be fine

at work tomorrow.

Practically midnight
blustery and boisterous
overconfident and churlish
drinks still in bottle
dances turned down
pills un-swallowed
thoughts awaiting birth
curfew broken
a paltry sleepless night
does not yet sting tired eyes.

Inventory of a Human Being

I've inventoried
books, furnace pipe,
cassette tapes, dishes,
matching socks,
baby shoes, teardrops,
lemons, earrings, and dog shampoo.

And thoughts.
I've inventoried those too
in full and painful detail.
Late at night, when I am alone
with the inside of my head
and those thoughts are not at all charitable.
Those I've wronged and what I've done
and those who've wronged me
and my perceptions
of what they've done.

The idea I keep coming back to
is that humans need
to count, to catalog
where we are
where we've been
where we're going.

These inventories
take a lot of precious effort and time
and while I'm counting out
my hours and days
and squandering thoughts -
about petty differences
and unimportant details -
I could be living without

a painstaking accounting
or the fear
of how much life
I may be allotted.

Childhood's Reflection

How Long, Not Long

How long childhood
not long, not long
changeable as the wind in March

      One moment
prickly, and skittish
given to bouts of wailing
the injustices
and the pain of trees
of humans, birds, and rocks
      The next
giggles and kisses
tight hugs, requests
for popsicles and skates
twirls like a fairy
you alighted in our lives

How you longed for the shock of freedom
that cool breeze that brings chills
notions and fancies
approaching softly on tiptoes
to whisper inspiration

Strummed lightly and hesitantly at first
that reverberation
bright vibration
harness that angst, god those days
why, oh why, didn't we
make note
of every whim and utterance

Nearly five hundred sixty-eight million
seconds in childhood

if we're graced
all those chances and choices
if we add them up
fleetingly, fleetingly
how long
to cradle and hug to our breast
how long, not long.

Loneliness and Imagination

A lonely childhood
can be a pebble tossed
into silent sacred pools -
those ripples created
escapes to places
if you allowed yourself
to be released
from mundane bondage
the everyday and the plain -
do you remember
sitting in the classroom
on a hot afternoon
at two fifty-five
it was so taxing
when all that was required
was a tiny peek out windows
to distant galaxies and beyond
your imagination
was wild
free and roaming
parts unknown
when you were a child
and loneliness
your key to awakening.

Birds and Bees

When I was four
I explained
the birds and the bees
succinctly and innocently
to my family
at the dinner table.

I'd been playing
at my friend's
house that day
She was six
and showed me
with her
Barbie and Ken Dolls
how to do *the* deed.

There we sat,
my family of five
me in my booster seat
because I was little
I used the word *fucking*
on Salmon Loaf Night
squished my hands together
to emulate what my friend
had told me.

Dead silence
mouths agape
then siblings' nervous laughter
followed shortly
sound spanking
delivered
by apoplectic father

I was merely
passing along information
I thought the family needed
my punishment -
a case of
shooting the messenger
if I'm being honest

And I knew
at that moment
I'd love that word
totally and completely
'til the day I die
a-men.

Fourth of July

Running, screeching delight
squish and splash
water balloons burst
precursor to later
thrills that frighten.

Bomb Pop, Big Stick
Orange Dreamsicle
everything felt
more special
like parade day.

Pavement
still hot
even after sundown
on bare feet
tiny rocks and grit gouged
real pain for a real day.

Safe spot to run
on grass
cool my soles
ever-present threat
banana slugs and other darkness
aunt and uncle's
on 4th of July.

Big fireworks - gonna get lit
and you-know-who's
illicit firecrackers
there's bound to be penance due.

Colors and sounds

beautiful and terrible
kaleidoscopes of experience
layered in my brain,
smell of
burning fuses,
hose at the ready
expectations high alert.

And the chaos
whistling, cracking, popping
only eclipsed
by a vanilla ice cream cone.

Summer Evenings

Hand-me-downs
not always shameful
instead—imaginations
made from steel
secure welds, chain link,
deathtrap engineering

Careful children -
we never wore helmets
and sakes alive,
in some of us, it shows.

Mom would preach,
don't fall on your teeth
her warnings were our
protective gear
and it seemed to work.

Teeter-totters, whirlwinds, swing-sets
they and we
cast-offs from the atomic age
iron curtain sensibilities
even the Troubles
were not
strong enough to withstand
everything the neighborhood kids
could serve up after school
Cold War Crisis
camouflaged as
glasnost and perestroika.

We were progeny of moon landings
and astronauts -

Space Camp
if our daddy was rich -
we played football in the street
raced our metal-wheeled skates
up and down the sidewalk
and drove the block to madness.

Innocence and evil doings
assassinations and protest marches
and I remember
being so proud
of my handsome cousin Bobby
in his dress sailor blues.

We asked the right questions
how could some of us be so free
while others were repressed
but they wanted us
to ignore the disparity -
anything uncomfortable
deemed impolite
still overlooked today
by politicians and talking heads
on the 5o'clock news.

Expecting Company

I am not sitting still
my legs dangle, swing
off the dining room chair.

I am waiting impatiently
for company to arrive
and festivities
to commence.

We did not have parties
at our house very often
there were other homes
bigger and fancier
with tastier food.

But here I was
sitting, waiting
tasked to be quiet
out of the way
do not scuff shoes
or rumple dress
which had been
starched and ironed.

I am waiting excitedly
with knot in my throat
butterflies in stomach
the end of my nose itches
I am trying to ignore it.

I must be well behaved
with perfect manners
I breathe

unsuccessfully silently
holding my anticipation in check.

Breathe In

Breathe in
fabric
sizing
likely toxic
nonetheless,
the fondest scent
of childhood -
material akin
to kisses from you
if I want them now
I know what to do

Breathe in
freshly laundered
gingham, corduroy,
dotted Swiss,
chenille,
now iron
and starch
those seams
fold precisely
into the cedar chest
for use another day

Breathe in
these things I know
about you now
and hold them
in my heart
things you kept hidden
to protect me
and to protect yourself
from memories that scarred -

kiss me goodnight
with all your heart and soul.

Mother Earth

Soon Transformed

Soon…
there'll come a day
when I'll wake up
and the weather will have changed
Summer will have gone
and with it those long days I love
Autumn will have turned
into nothing but a memory
like leaves fallen
from my liquid amber
then - I'll feel the Winter
deep in my bones
that time for chilled sleep
and shivers
from the mountains
the smell of sugar-pine pitch
cold air has a secret scent
and Spring seems to have
the hardest job
pushing and birthing
bursting forth into new life
and blossoms
Soon…

Blackbirds

I am
a gentle
persistent
fixation of taxonomy
of avian variety -
from earliest years
I watched blackbirds
their red-tipped wings
and sailing notes
I plucked
from my guitar
given my druthers
maybe I'll come back next life
and take to the skies
with the blackbirds
flying free.

How a Fish Sees

Think about
the poor fish gasping
for his life
not gasping for air
extracting it from water
his eyes bulging
they seem unmoved
(by my encroaching
upon his morning swim)
still, they must be sighted

What I wonder
is how does a fish see?
do his optic nerves
behave the same way as
do mine? I ponder this
but I am not
scientific in nature.

Back to our breathless fish -
I'd hooked him in the river
but he was small and not
quite right for supper -
so I threw him back
let him swim in the sun
and grow a bit longer.

Before I was back
and bothering him again
I also hoped that maybe
he'd be too clever in the future
to get tangled with my hook
or anyone else's

I wanted him to live
to ripe old fish-age -
do you understand?

Sweeping the Clouds

Upward
sky-born psalms
and feed my
benediction
your shapes
I'm sure are miracles
scattered over
heaven's distant fields.

Virga curtain fantasy
draws down upon our joy
it changes to a soggy beacon
of every when I've spied.

Crossing close
feathered cirrus
angel's wings drift
tickling eyelids and my fancy.

What do you think is hiding -
just behind the folly
fantastic lenticular scene
that stretches across
whole mountain tops
as though it is a dream.

We'll rest, my love
upon our backs
in fields of poppies
and sweet clover
hurry do,
please don't be late
see what the clouds reveal

Pirate ship or mastodon
waves on an infinite ocean
witch, tiger, ballerina,
horse and carriage
these soaked tea leaves
at the bottom of a cup.

Every shape unique
and bares a fine inspection
look fast before scenes disappear
for the simple pleasures we might find
in clouds that sweep across the sky.

Brooding Balance

When storms
crash in upon me
I let nature match the mood
and move me through
these brooding feelings
of my darkened thoughts.

I need to be in the mountains
to feel the menacing sky
wind raging at trees in violence
and ghostly strains of distant
locomotive sounds.

To stand in awe and silence
wrinkling my nose in recognition
as ozone quickens the air
as if it's just as anxious as I
and feel as static fills my hair.

The rain begins
mouth opens wide
and I drink fat drops
a few at a time
then it comes down in torrents
and I must escape
or surely I shall drown.

My legs are splashed
by the mud where I stand
arms open in sweet supplication
I offer myself
to this chaotic day
nature, do me a kind turn, I pray
it is the way I wait for balance.

Ashes Scattered

Ashes blowing
raining a terrible storm
stirred into everything
acrid reminders of where I live

I learned how to fear
those deeply planted horrors
before I ever came to be
but I never felt that way about a fire

Fireplace memories and bonfires
for cooking, for warmth
nostalgia - all the scattered thoughts
of glowing eyes, bodies, and hearts

Fire becomes fear - mother goddess wakes
nature has her way with me
Kali devastates - build and grow
I weep damaged sorrow

Ashes blowing
four winds thrown
I tremble at her greatness, her speed
anticipating a different kind of burn

Rebirth and new growth I do not see
I only think about the ashes
smoke clogging throat and burning eyes
worlds turned upside down in an instant.

Season's Cycle

I live in patterns
and not patterns.

I awaken to star shine
gentle moon glow
it's all just half light
then bright sunshine
always whispering
dark hallways
quietly crept down
wooden stairways.

Glorious spring emotions
earth and water
downpour then gentle rain
plant and grow and watch
let us be new to one another
I desire strawberry plants
and to feed birds
watch sweet peas invade my front yard
marvel at how
even the tenderest of things
thrive after such a bad winter.

I live in summer denial
Fahrenheit memory
stinging heat and lassitude
ennui mimicking heartbeats
an indolent desire
of bees humming
sweat runs down back
always praying
strange weather

take me home
to my regularly scheduled life
at any moment.

How you then wake one day
and you know
with every fiber of your being
it is autumn
it happens gloriously
wind gusts and screams
down the valleys, through the hills
naptime and create time, dream time
it is absolutely time for soup.

I never know
when it's going to be winter
until it's too late
get out of the icy wind
it evokes balance and behavior.
go walking in the cold - smell the mountains
though they are miles up the hill
they still find you, those mountains
and remind you who you are.

Season's cycle
internal directives and influences
Mother Nature's whims
gifts from the goddess.

Dandelion

I loved blowing dandelion seeds
        to the breezes
And my mother never told me no
I did this with impunity
        until, one day
While at my papa's house
        there was one hiding innocently
        on the edge of the lawn out back
So I plucked it none too carefully
        put it to my lips and blew
Papa scolded me gently
Now there'd be dandelions growing
        rampant
        in his yard and down the block
Imagine a child my age responsible
        for all those dandelions
I was delighted—
He was not.

Are you a dandelion lover—
Or do you relegate this stalwart plant
To the weed bin.

Here's a secret about me:
When I'm gardening, sometimes
        I uproot the little dears
        just like my papa did
But sometimes—
I make sure no one's looking
        I pluck a good healthy one
        with lots of fluff
        and blow.

Rainbow Elegance

There's an elegance
to a rainbow
that magically fades before
you're even quite sure
you actually saw it.

Mine today
was broad and bright
each color so distinct -
at its beginning
becoming lighter and lighter
beyond memory
towards its end.

Is it true
do you think
that there's something
of a miracle
in this refraction of light
and vapors
and sunshine?

Some spectral beauty
causing me to feel lucky
when a rainbow
makes its presence known
on a drive
in the mountains
just this side of a rainstorm.

I realized it's been
too, too long
since I'd seen a rainbow last

what have I become
that I've forgotten
when majesty is at play.

Songs of the Birds

I listen
to birds
when they visit
and wonder
if they hear
themselves
how sweet their sound
and do they notice mine
or is my voice wretched
a dark and distant
refrain
a guttural language
in which they have no interest
do I sound an inner alarm
making terrible vibrations
and how do they move about
so composedly
when I loom as close as I can
to hear their tender song.

Graceless

I will never say a bird is graceless
Even when it is just starting out
Leaving nest for the first time
I say that it is just learning.

First, it tries.
Then, it does.
And, it is.

It rises, moves, and dips
On warm air currents
with an arc and arch of wings
Blood and feathers, bones, skin, and muscle perfectly
Synchronized with
Things it is to be
And in divine harmony with
Unafraid of flying or falling or dying.

And it tries.
And it does.
And it is.

If I could, I would
I'd wish -
I'd be more like them
Let my feet follow the directive
And stretch and imagine I had
The wings to fly
I'd arc and arch
Into the feelings of my own story.

I would learn.
And do.

And be.

Stop the worry,
Of being in this momentary world
Even if I am graceless.
Allow me to become -
Whatever it is I will become.

Red Tailed Hawks

Red-tailed hawks
circle warm currents
choose their home
tree-top site perhaps
for the next few years
if all goes well

I didn't see you build your nest
but I noticed you
traveling to and fro
and realized through
binoculars
that you had babies

Two eggs hatched and
the feeding began
duties split between parents
Papa hunts while Mama
rips meat to shreds
the babies eat hungrily

Do you feel at one with nature
the earth and with each other
is it only humans who desperately define
and refine their views and importance
I know this truth too well
and I see infinite beauty reflected in your eyes

Weeks go by and then flight
and I watch with rapt attention
as fledglings try their wings
and build their skills
mother and father still

feeding them as they grow

In strength and speed
hunting, drifting on the air
diving, playing
and the cycle continues
it won't be long now
before they leave the nest

Certainly, birds feel time pass
differently from humans
but still, I quietly wonder
how things are for the parents
when their youngsters leave the nest.

Sensible Flowers

Isn't it amazing
that flowers
know just what to do?

To push toward the sunlight
and show themselves in the
most beautiful ways possible

Do you wonder
if their grandparents and parents
and aunts and uncles, too
schooled them -
please peony, bachelor button,
French lavender, bearded iris, butterfly weed
and portulaca -
be sensible children
let the right bees pollinate
pay attention
in school
and guard against the dangers
for there are many.

One day,
if you're lucky,
your stems and stamens and petals
will be the most glorious things to grow from
our little patch of dirt.

Sweet Refreshment

I bite
and summer juices
drip in rivulets
down my laughing face
making sweet mess of me
this luscious treat
no matter how often I partake
or how old I become
this feels of the most sinful, perfect luxury
rites of solstice
peaches speak of true love
apricots sate like the sun
plums as sweet as your ripe lips
working into the most beautiful grin
let me taste, just a taste
for that moment of sweet refreshment
my entire being craves.

Underwater Shimmer

We stood at lake's edge
watching last moments
of a lovely day
fish still jumping
gobbling mosquitoes
      it had started to rain
but there were still glints
here and there
of weakened sunlight
amongst darkening clouds and sky
shimmering over the mostly quiet water
      what do you think?
she asked
      no idea
we replied
then speculation
      a cloud
      school of fish
      monster from lake's floor
just below the surface, a shadow
roughly five feet in diameter
      did it move or sit stationary?
we couldn't even answer
the most basic of questions
it was certainly magical
then it dispersed
we never found out
and the rain came down
mixing smells
petrichor, wood smoke, pavement, ozone
      the rain changed things
we took our small adventure
added it to our memories together.

Rock in the Riverbed

This river swells, flows
rushes and brambles grow
down to the water line
sun glints
teeming with life
songbirds recite psalms

what is this place
existing as it does
on the other side of the world
a place I've never been
how still it stands
in my mind's eye

it was just
a photograph shared
colors sharp, so real
they offered to swallow me whole
scent of clean - stings
and stretches
a wishing

it is the origin story I am in love with
the idea that everything has a starting place
and I am obsessed
with the beginnings of things

brand new book
first bike
chance meetings
new box of crayons
first cup of coffee
that kiss

new friend

heady and marvelous
that is not to say
things already in existence
are tarnished and lacking relevance
always can find room
to blend old with new
and I decorate my life
with ancient relics
right alongside
new ideas
new ways of being
and perhaps now
I am the ancient relic
oldest rock in the riverbed
but still I long for the headwaters
that first sweet sip
that bubbles from the ground
a wellspring
and I will taste this magic

endings are where things become tricky
and where I'll see the stuff of which I'm made.

Offerings

Hot dry sand
loose, larger bits
small stones
sea grass
fishing line
smoothed wood
this is no bed
of hot coals
run for it
gull feather remnant
broken shell bit
exoskeletal
something or other
sparkles
ah, sea glass
feet burn
squeaky terrain
dry kelp whips
seaweed wands
sand size smaller
brain praises
tactile changes
shore birds squawk
waves crash
breezes temper
sands blistering
damp relief
closer, closer
blissful edge
salty waves merge
toes stretch
up and out
sun salutation

feet in charge
further in
farther out
ocean purity
tactile offerings
give it all back
Amphitrite and Poseidon.

Author's Note

Here I am again, and I have not stopped writing poems. When I wrote *Bird with a Bright Object*, I didn't know where it would lead or that I was even on any sort of road. I only remember being nervous about letting you see my inner self. So much so, that I held off publishing the work for eleven months after that manuscript was completed.

This time around, the process had different challenges. I wondered if you would enjoy the poems to the same degree as the first book. I hope they feel like a grand adventure. Let them take you places you've never been and places you've always dreamed of visiting. Please try them on for size and see how they fit.

There is always a price to be paid for exposing vulnerability, but I think it was worth every bit of my creative angst. Best therapy, ever, at least; that's what I tell myself.

I loved writing this batch of poems and am so pleased to share them with you. It is a privilege for me to set them free.

From my heart –

AmyLee

Acknowledgements

When it was time for me to edit this book of poetry, I asked for help, and the wonderful people listed below showed up for me. They all have way better things to do in their spare time, so I feel extremely fortunate that they were willing to read my poems. If they have an asterisk by their name, it means I've managed to charm them twice.

*Ticia Isom, *Richard Holeman, *Heather Wickers, David Owen Thompson, Alex Dresner, Jailyn James, Annie B., Joe Garland, Anne Waldon.

I'm grateful for their diligence, keen eyes, and kindness. Each brings a little something different and magical to the table. If I could, I would hug them all. Instead, I will say thank you kindly.

Kat of Katherine Magpie Design created the cover, and Jourdan Dunn did the formatting interior design of the book. It was so great to work with them again, and I feel lucky to know I can trust their words and their work. Beautiful job, you guys!

About the Author

Whether it's raw verses filled with the grit of life and love, laments about lost family, or sacred offerings about the natural world, AmyLee writes with her whole heart. She has worked in the book and publishing world for decades and now spends her days learning the craft of writing and supporting independent authors as they refine their work.

AmyLee lives in the Foothills of California with her husband. She's a long-time member of the Sonora Writers' Group and has belonged to multiple book clubs over the years. She sometimes hosts a poetry show on Twitter Spaces, *The Poetry Show with AmyLee*. You can find some of AmyLee's poetry and short fiction pieces at:
https://medium.com/@amylee_53969